Promoting Positive Racial Teacher Student Classroom Relationships: Methodology

Other Works by Dr. Derrick L. Campbell

Books
- *Promoting Positive Racial Teacher Student Classroom Relationships*
- *Promoting Positive Racial Teacher Student Classroom Relationships: Workbook*
- *Leading Your Marriage into the Promised Land*
- *Leading Your Marriage into the Promised Land: Workbook for Husbands*
- *Leading Your Marriage into the Promised Land: Workbook for Wives*
- *Advanced Marriage Training for Singles*

Education Articles
- *Cultural Influences: Differences in Teacher Perspectives*
- *Developing Student Recognition Programs for Historically Underserved Students*
- *Ethical Leadership Develops Moral Communities*
- *Firing the Principal Does Not Guarantee Improvement*
- *Leadership Qualities that Promote Positive Racial Teacher-Student Relationships*
- *Poverty: The Assumed Link to Low Minority Student Achievement*
- *Reducing Cultural Bullying in Schools*
- *Reducing Cultural Challenges Saves Money*
- *Reducing Inappropriate Special Education Referrals for Historically Underserved Students*
- *Save Money by Reducing Student Suspensions*
- *Smile: They Like It*
- *Steering the Organizational Change Process*
- *Student Input is the Key to Effective Classroom Management*
- *Student Perspectives of Classroom Disruptions*
- *Students Need Professional Development Too*
- *Students Who Promote Positive Racial Teacher-Student Classroom Relationships: Part 1*
- *Students Who Promote Positive Racial Teacher-Student Classroom Relationships: Part 2*
- *Teacher Perspectives of Classroom Disruptions*
- *Teacher Qualities that Promote Positive Racial Classroom Relationships*
- *Transforming Afro-American Content into the School Curriculum*
- *Unions Can Benefit Organizational Change*
- *Classroom Management Strategies*

Promoting Positive Racial Teacher Student Classroom Relationships: Methodology

The Step-by-Step Plan for Successful Implementation

Dr. Derrick L. Campbell, Ed.D.

DLC Consultant Group

Published by Derrick L. Campbell

First edition: April 2015

ISBN: 978-0-9802039-3-6

Printed in the United States of America

TABLE OF CONTENTS

ABOUT THE AUTHOR

Dr. Campbell holds a Bachelor of Science degree in Electronics Engineering Technology from Capital Institute of Technology, a second Bachelor of Science degree in Math Education from the University of the District of Columbia, a Masters in Education Administration from Lincoln University, and a doctoral degree in Educational Leadership from Rowan University.

He is also the founder and CEO of DLC Consultant Group. After authoring his first book, *Promoting Positive Racial Teacher-Student Classroom Relationships*, in January 2008, Dr. Campbell developed a Cultural Relationship Training Program that improves teacher-student classroom relationships as well as several companion programs. He also developed the B.O.S.S. Leadership Training Program that improves manager-employee workplace relationships and relationships between Law Enforcement and their local community.

Dr. Campbell authored his second book, *Leading Your Marriage into the Promised Land,* in February 2009. *Leading Your Marriage into the Promised Land* educates the husband on a leadership process that ensures the husband and wife work together as a team. The husband and wife work together to develop and implement agreed upon goals that embrace the different values that they learn as children. Following the writing of this book, he wrote two companion workbooks, one for husbands and the other for wives.

Dr. Campbell authored his fifth book - *Advanced Marriage Training for Singles* - in September, 2014. *Advanced Marriage Training for Singles* better equips singles to make informed decisions about who they marry before they decide to become engaged.

Dr. Campbell is founder and president of The Promised Land Ministry. The Promised Land Ministry provides training for churches, non-profit organizations, men, and couples. Churches and non-profit organizations receive training in the areas of strategic planning, team building, and leadership.

In August 2007, Dr. Campbell founded Leadership Advancement Journal which publishes articles on recent educational, organizational, and business developments that impact our culture. His articles, Reducing Cultural Bullying in Schools and Reducing Inappropriate Special Education Referrals for Historically Underserved Students, have been featured in a local New Jersey newspaper.

In November 2008, Dr. Campbell began the new Radio talk show - Culturally Speaking with Doctor Derrick. On this talk show we discuss the solutions to the cultural challenges that exist in our schools, workplaces, and community. Dr. Campbell has had a host of local and national speakers who contributed to the content of the show.

Dr. Campbell has lectured at various locations throughout the nation, including the National Association for the Advancement of Colored People (NAACP), Iron Sharpens Iron Men's Conference, and local churches. He has ministered to the youth at his home church on the topic of Christian student rights in the public schools and has ministered at another local New Jersey church on Overcoming the Poverty Cycle. He has been a board member of his church's men's ministry, Athletes United in

Christ, and has participated in various church activities. He has facilitated Leading Your Marriage into the Promised seminars at churches and the Iron Sharpens Iron Conference Men's Conference.

LIST OF FIGURES

LIST OF TABLES

Table   Page

INTODUCTION

During my twenty years of education, I have seen many careers destroyed due to allegations of racism. Once there is an allegation of racism, the perception of the teacher and the school is changed forever. I have realized that educators must ask themselves: How do I protect myself or my school district from the problems associated with alleged claims of racism?

The biggest problem associated with claims of racism is the perception that students and parents have regarding teachers and schools. Many of the complaints surface as opposition to over disciplining children in the classroom and schools. The opposition continues and when the problem is not remedied to the satisfaction of the student or parent then local civil rights entities become involved or the parent files a complaint with the United States Department of Education Office of Civil rights. Involvement at this level end with the media broadcasting the complaint and now the racial allegation becomes a bigger problem. The best way to offset allegations of racism is to transform the gap between the students perception of the teachers intentions by promoting positive racial teacher student classroom relationships.

Educators who promote positive racial teacher student classroom relationships will empower teachers to work together as a team to protect themselves as well as the school from the negative perception associated with allegations of racism. Additionally, positive relationships at schools and in the classroom are in many ways the prerequisites for effective learning and behavior.

Developing positive relationships with students provides benefits for schools, teachers, and students. Having positive and caring relationships in schools increases resilience and protects children from academic failure, mental illness, drug and alcohol abuse, and destructive behavior and violence. Long-term teacher-student relationships result in increased teacher job satisfaction. Teachers who have positive feelings toward their students are more likely to have students reciprocate those positive feelings. Teachers who develop positive and personal relationships with students may prevent psychological development problems in their students.

Students believe their academic achievement increases when they have positive relationships with teachers.

Learn the step-by-step process for empowering teachers to transform the gap between the students perceptions of teacher intentions. Learn that process by reading this book today!

METHODOLOGY

Discrimination against marginalized students is a persistent problem in classrooms throughout the United States (Garcia, 1984) that can influence classroom relationships between minority students and White teachers. Teachers can devastate teacher-student relationship development by bringing cultural incompatibilities into the classroom (Ornstein & Levine, 1990). White teachers may have difficulty motivating and understanding minority students due to differences in dialect and language, refusal to accept the learning capabilities of working-class students, and rejection of minority students' lifestyle and culture. Whites may bring cultural differences that cause many classroom discipline problems for minority students.

The educational process in classrooms includes verbal communication between students and teachers (Borich, 1986; Good, 1983; Morganett, 1991; Rosenshine, 1983; Sava, 2002; Wassermann, 1992). Minority students exhibit verbal and classroom behavior that White teachers may consider offensive and counterproductive to the educational process. Puerto Ricans make decisions jointly where one person speaks and others join in and respond until a decision is made (Milburn, 2000). Black children are inclined to talk back when motivated by what a teacher says (Gay, 1975). Urban Black students argue for recognition of unsuccessful efforts toward completing a task (Gilbert & Gay, 1985). Blacks verbally communicate by telling the truth or telling it like it is. Black communities view truth-telling or telling-it-like-it-is verbal communication as courageous, honest, and refusing-to-compromise integrity. Anglo European cultures view this communication process as confrontational (Shade et al., 1997).

Confrontational minority student classroom behavior can result from the perspectives minorities have regarding learning. Involuntary minorities, such as Blacks, are not willing to perform well in school due to difficulty in crossing cultural lines (Ogbu, 1992). Mexican American children attempt to learn collectively and maximize their intellectual exchange and knowledge acquisition by working together on assignments, which may result in Mexican American students copying answers from each other (Shade, 1997). "When Black students are forced to separate only the cognitive component for use in the classroom, they feel that this is unnatural and find it difficult to honor the teacher's request" (Gilbert & Gay, 1985, p. 135). Before Black students begin a task, they may look over the assignment in its entirety, rearrange their posture and writing space, ask the teacher to repeat the directions, check the perception of other neighboring students, and check their pencils and paper (Gilbert & Gay, 1985). For Black students, these are necessary classroom behaviors while teachers may perceive the students are inattentive, disruptive, or not prepared, or attempting to avoid completing the task (Gilbert & Gay, 1985). Blacks learn question-and-answer sessions result when an adult is angry with them, and this process may inhibit students from classroom involvement (Bennett, 1997). When teachers require only cognitive activities, Black students feel the request is unnatural and have difficulty following the teacher's request, which results in frustration and withdrawal for Black students (Gay, 1975). Blacks have a low tolerance for monotonous or low-level activity, and prefer and need a constant change of information coupled with a variety of information (Boykin, 1979).

Minority classroom behaviors could present challenges for White teachers, which might result in classroom discipline problems. Many discipline problems improve when teachers and students develop positive interactive relationships (Chappell & McCoy, 2003). According to Kearney (1984), students and teachers who are warm, compassionate, and friendly toward one another in the classroom have the potential to improve instruction and learning. Students are more likely to complete assignments in classes where they feel accepted by the teacher (Morganett, 1991). Acceptance and approval from the teacher in a school setting may enhance student self-esteem and self-evaluation (Sava, 2002).

Minority students and teachers at Sunny Shade High School (SSHS) have relationship challenges that devalue students and reject the culture they bring to the school setting. After analyzing student discipline data, I found that teacher-student interactions account for 70% of the discipline referrals at SSHS (Sunny Shade High School, 2006). The SSHS teaching staff is 95% White, and the student population is 93% minority. These racial dynamics may be the source of the significant percentage discipline referrals, indicating that teacher and student interactions need improvement. Therefore, the purpose of this participatory action research project is to promote positive racial teacher-student classroom relationships.

Research Questions

The research questions for this study were:

1) How does my leadership promote positive racial teacher-student classroom relationships at SSHS?

2) What impact does promoting positive racial teacher-student classroom relationships at SSHS have on school discipline and student achievement?

3) What strategies can teachers and students use to promote positive racial teacher-student classroom relationships?

Design of the Study

The design of the study was a participatory action research project. Participatory action research is a collaborative social process in which people join together to plan a change by studying, reframing, and reconstructing social processes that deliberately liberate people from unjust or unproductive social experiences (Kemmis & McTaggert, 2005). Participatory action research is a reflective process in which the researcher participates in a deliberative process that transforms his or her practices through a spiral of cycles and self-critical action and reflection by exploring the potential of different perspectives, theories, or discourses. Participatory action research provides researchers with the opportunity to develop multiple strategies that can solve educational challenges.

Participatory action researchers reflect to understand their practices as they emerge within their own social circumstances, and participatory action is a recursive process that begins with planning a change, acting or observing change processes and consequences, and reflecting on the change processes and consequences (Kemmis & McTaggert, 2005). The participatory action research model provides a paradigm that guided me to reflect on my leadership as I planned, observed, participated in, and reflected on a change process that will promote positive racial teacher-student classroom relationships.

This participatory action research project used a concurrent transformative research design. Concurrent transformative research design is a mixed methods research study that combines qualitative and quantitative approaches in the research methodology of a single study or multiphased study by using concurrent or sequential data collection and analysis strategies that integrate data at one or more stages in the research process (Cresswell, 2003; Tashakkori & Teddlie, 2003). Mixed methods research designs provide researchers with multiple strategies that enable the researcher to engage in the participatory action research project.

Mixed methods studies originated with pragmatists such as Charles Sanders Peirce (1839–1914), William James (1842–1910), George Herbert Mead (1863–1931), John Dewey (1859–1952), and Author Bentley (1870–1957) (Tashakkori & Teddlie, 2003). These researchers conceptualized mixed methods ideology by rejecting the assumption that scientific inquiry is accomplished by a single scientific method. Charles Pierce introduced a scientific research method that included three phases— the observer object, the working scientist, and the signs scientist—that he used to understand, describe, and explain this world. William James incorporated Pierce's scientific research method into his psychological and paranormal phenomena research. George Mead, a colleague of John Dewey, influenced psychologists and social scientists with a three-part methodology research project on social behaviorisms. Author Bentley influenced political science by presenting the concept of government as a process. "Dewey sought to invest social science with more objective methods within the larger concerns of people as they formed communities" (Tashakkori & Teddlie, 2003, p. 53). World War I and the American financial depression in the 1930s caused universities to replace pragmatism with analytical philosophical research until the 1960s (Tashakkori & Teddlie, 2003). According to Tashakkori and Teddlie (2003):

> A neo-pragmatic period began during the late 1960's and fueled a wholly new way of thinking about pragmatism and its place in philosophy, science, and life, making pragmatism as much a

philosophy and method of research as it is a

political, religious, and aesthetic statement. (p. 53)

Campbell and Fiske (1959) encouraged others to use the mixed methods approach after conducting a study that validated psychological traits. Researchers have benefited from using mixed methods ideology by developing and implementing research strategies that were considered abnormal.

Mixed methods studies provide researchers with benefits not established in traditional research models. According to Teddlie and Tashakkori (2003), traditional quantitative and qualitative methods have limited effectiveness when used individually. Traditional research methods provide biases by focusing exclusively on the culture of the respondents and neglecting research discipline culture and researcher culture (Tashakkori & Teddlie, 2003). According to Moghaddam, Walker, and Harré (2003), the traditional research view suggests that laboratory and experimental research completely separates the culture of respondents, research, and researcher while ethnography completely infuses respondent, research, and researcher culture into the study. Researchers have employed mixed method approaches after recognizing that single method use has limitations that can create cultural and individual biases (Cresswell, 2003; Tashakkori & Teddlie, 2003). Mixed methods enable the researcher to verify and generate theory in the same study by answering confirmatory and exploratory study questions (Tashakkori & Teddlie, 2003). Cresswell (2003) reports that mixed methods involve (a) determining implementation sequence, (b) prioritizing data collection and analysis, (c) determining data integration stage, and (d) using an overall theoretical perspective. Mixed methods provide the researcher an opportunity to use an overall theoretical perspective, such as participatory action research, while integrating qualitative and quantitative research methods, such as concurrent transformative design, that verify and generate theory without biases that could have contaminated the study.

Mixed methods can serve a transformative purpose that emphasizes advocacy or change for marginalized groups such as women, ethnic minorities, people with disabilities, and the poor (Mertens, 2003). Participatory action research involves transforming theory and practices that advocate change for marginalized groups (Kemmis & McTaggert, 2005). Concurrent transformative research designs are guided by theoretical perspectives such as critical theory, advocacy, and participatory action research (Tashakkori & Teddlie, 2003). Therefore, the participatory action research project employed mixed methods consistent with concurrent transformative research design.

The concurrent transformative research design included a concurrent mixed model and monostrand research models. Concurrent procedures require researchers to collect qualitative and quantitative data in the same time frame in order to provide a comprehensive research analysis (Cresswell, 2003). According to Tashakkori & Teddlie, (2003), concurrent transformative designs:

may employ qualitative, quantitative, or mixed methods so long as the ideological lens of advocacy or participation is a central element in shaping the purpose, the questions, the collaborative nature of data collection and analysis, and the interpreting and reporting of results. (p. 232)

Figure 1 shows that a concurrent mixed model design is a study that has separate strands of research purposes or questions. Each strand has a data type, analysis, and inferences. Both inferences are combined to develop a metainference (Tashakkori & Teddlie, 2003). Figure 2 reveals a monostrand design is a study with research questions that include data collection, data analysis, and an inference. A monostrand study includes explanatory or confirmatory research purposes or questions that use qualitative or quantitative research methods to answer research questions and makes qualitative or quantitative inferences (Tashakkori & Teddlie, 2003). The researcher used several qualitative and quantitative research strategies in the concurrent mixed model and monostrand research design.

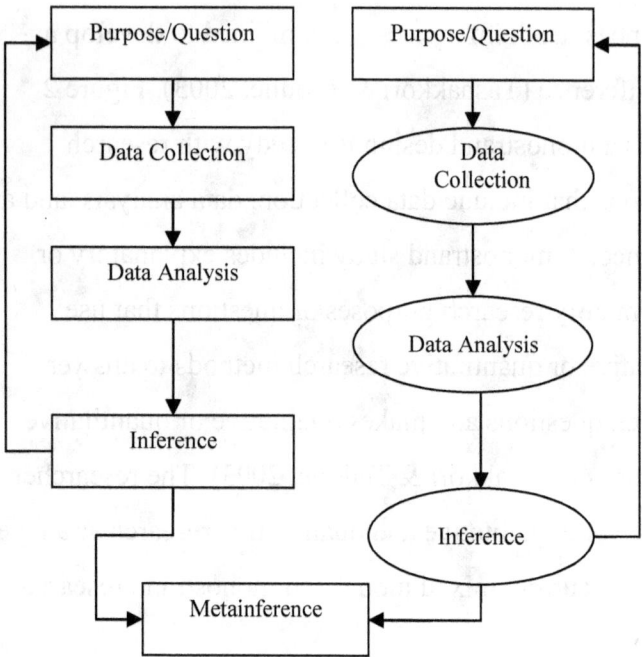

Figure 1 Concurrent mixed model

Taken from Tashakkori & Teddlie, 2003, p. 688

```
┌─────────────────────────┐
│     Purpose/Question     │
└─────────────────────────┘
            │
            ▼
┌─────────────────────────┐
│     Data Collection      │
└─────────────────────────┘
            │
            ▼
┌─────────────────────────┐
│      Data Analysis       │
└─────────────────────────┘
            │
            ▼
┌─────────────────────────┐
│        Inference         │
└─────────────────────────┘
```

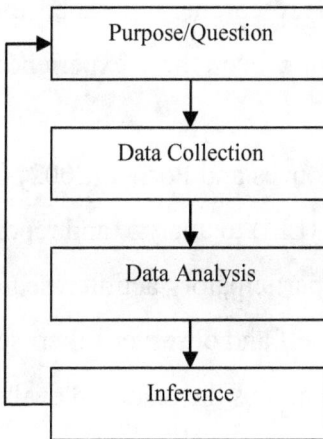

Figure 2 Monostrand research design.

Taken from Tashakkori & Teddlie, 2003, p. 684

The procedure for leadership data acquisition in this participatory action research project was an autoethnography. An autoethnography is the study of "one's own culture and oneself as part of that culture" (Patton, 2002, p. 85). Culture is collective behavior patterns and beliefs that represent standards for deciding (a) what is, (b) what can be, (c) how one feels about it, and (d) how to go about doing it (Goodenough, 1971). In an autoethnography, the researcher reports his experiences with a culture and reflects on these experiences (Patton, 2002).

I used the Kouzes and Posner (2002) Leadership Practices Inventory (LPI) to analyze and report leader participation in the participatory action research project. The LPI includes a self and observer Likert scale survey. The LPI self survey allows the leader to evaluate his leadership characteristics. The observer survey allow manger, colleagues, coworkers, and other the opportunity to supply feedback regarding the leader.

Setting

SSHS is located in Sunny Shade County. The demographics for Sunny Shade City reveal that most persons are Black (53.3%), Hispanic (38.8%), White (16.8%), Asian (2,5%) and others (3.9%) (U.S. Census, 2006). The median household income in Sunny Shade City was $23,421, per capita income was less than $10,000, and fewer than 36% of the population was the below the poverty line. Ninety-five percent of the students who attend SSHS reside in Sunny Shade City.

SSHS has an organizational structure similar to other public school districts. Table 1 reveals that most school employees are White personnel with the exception of cafeteria and student workers. SSHS offers curricular, noncurricular, and athletic activities for all students.

Table 1

SSHS Staff Demographics

School occupation	Ethnicity percentage		
	Black	Hispanic	White
Administrator	33	0	67
Teaching staff	3	2	95
Office staff	10	20	70
Technical instructors	0	0	100
Ancillary personnel	0	0	100
Technicians	0	0	100
Cafeteria workers	60	0	40
Student workers	29	71	0

Students who attend SSHS come from various demographic backgrounds. The total student population was 706 students. Student gender composition is 53% female and 47% male. Student ethnic backgrounds included Hispanic (60%), Black (33%), White (4%), and Asian Pacific Islander (3%). Ninety-nine percent of the students qualify for reduced or free lunch. Grade-level student demographics included ninth graders (24%), 10th graders (28%), 11th graders (24%), and 12th graders (24%).

Data Collection Strategies

Qualitative and quantitative data collection strategies for this participatory action research project included individual interviews, focus group interviews, classroom observations, document collection, surveys, and digital journaling. Including various data collection strategies provided me with multiple data collection methods. Multiple data collection methods increase trustworthiness and data validity (Glense, 2006; Patton, 2002).

I used interviews to collect qualitative data. Interviews provide the researcher with a real-life data collection process to assist the researcher with a study (Glense, 2006). Interviews provide researchers with information for academic analysis (Fontana & Frey, 2005). Interviews were structured and unstructured. In structured interviews, all interviewees receive the same set of questions in the same order, and then the responses are coded according to some preestablished scheme. Unstructured interviews are open-ended. Interviews provide researchers with a method to develop detailed holistic descriptions and processes that integrate multiple perspectives by reporting interrelated behaviors and events that bridge intersubjectives for reporting research as an insider and identifying and framing hypothesis for quantitative research (Weiss, 1994).

I tape-recorded interviews. Recording interviews provides the researcher the opportunity to transcribe interviewees' responses verbatim (Weiss, 1994). Each interviewee signed a consent form before the interview. I used an interview guide that provided me with guiding questions for the interview. Interview guides ensure the interviewer "has carefully decided how best to use limited time available in an interview situation" (Patton, 2002, p. 343). I formulated questions that parallel the first four Ladder of Inference rungs, which Argyris (1990) developed and Senge et al. (2000) expanded. Senge et al. (2000) expanded the Ladder of Inference to include (a) observable data and experiences, (b) selected data from observations, (c) added cultural and personal meanings, (d) assumptions made about cultural and personal beliefs, (e) conclusions, (f) adopted beliefs, and (g) actions taken based on those beliefs. After transcribing the interviews, I returned transcribed interview copies to each interviewee to verify the transcriptions and increase validity by member checking. Member checking involves sharing interview transcriptions with research participants to make sure the researcher represents them and their ideas (Glense, 2006).

Next, I facilitated focus group interviews. Focus group interviews are guided or unguided discussions regarding a specific topic of interest to a set of people and the researcher (Edmonds, 1999; Glense, 2006). Focus group discussions can include collecting data in a one-shot setting and facilitating collective brainstorming to solve problems (Berg, 2007). Focus group interviews enable a researcher to collect large quantities of data in a short time period, resulting in powerful insights that are not available with individual interviews (Kamberelis & Dimitriadis,

2005). Focus group interviews were a primary vehicle for collecting data from participating staff during this study.

I conducted classroom observations. Observations provided several advantages (Patton, 2002). Observations enable the researcher to depend less on preconceived notions that may inhibit learning things people may be unwilling to reveal. In addition, observations provided me with an opportunity to move beyond selective perceptions of others and permits formalizing an independent analysis. I recorded field notes from the observations for coding, analysis, and evaluation.

In addition to collecting field notes, I collected documents for qualitative and quantitative analysis. Document collection enables the researcher to understand the historical development related to the research topic (Glense, 2006) and report descriptive statistics using SSPS computer descriptive software. Descriptive software is a tool that helps to organize and summarize data (Holcomb, 1998). I used the SSPS statistical software program to evaluate student grades, student attendance, discipline resolution information, and discipline referral information.

Statistical software programs simplify quantitative data analysis by simplifying data entry and statistical examination without using formulas (Holcomb, 1998).

I analyzed and evaluated the observations, interviews, focus group interviews, and documents. Analyzing and evaluating observations, interviews, focus group interviews, and documents require coding. Coding, the first step of data analysis (Holstein & Gubruim, 2005; Patton, 2002), involves analyzing interviews and observations for essential content (Patton, 2002) as well as sorting and integrating materials (Cresswell, 1998; Weiss, 1994). Coding provides a link between the interviews, observations, and gathered documents (Weiss, 1994).

Finally, I used a survey and digital journaling to collect data regarding my leadership and used the Kouzes and Posner (2002) Leadership Practices Inventory (LPI). The LPI is a survey instrument that uses a software program to provide feedback regarding leadership behavior. The LPI includes a self and observer Likert scale survey. The Likert survey uses a scale from 1 to 10. Scale divisions are (a) almost never, (b) rarely, (c) seldom, (d) once in a while, (e) occasionally, (f) sometimes, (g) fairly often, (h) usually, (I) very frequently, and (j) almost always. I completed a 30-item self-assessment of the five components related to the Leadership Challenge. Participatory action research project participants and other staff members completed a 30-item leader observer survey. Additionally, I used a digital journal to record leadership reflections and activities.

Study Participants

The participants for this participatory action research project were students and teachers at SSHS. In Cycle 1, I interviewed eight teachers and eight students who have been involved in teacher-student interactions that led to classroom disruptions. I recruited teachers and students who volunteered to participate in the interviews. Table 3 reveals that most students who participated in the case study interviews were Hispanic females. Most teachers who participated in the case study interviews were White females. Teacher gender and ethnic demographics were White females (50%), White males (25%), Hispanic females (12.5%), and Black females (12.5%). Student gender and ethnic demographics were Hispanic males

(50%), Black females (25%), Hispanic females (12.5%), and Black males (12.5%).

Table 2

Case Study Participants' Demographics

	Gender		Ethnicity		
	Male	Female	Black	Hispanic	White
Students	25%	75%	25%	75%	0%
Teachers	50%	50%	12.5%	12.5%	75%

The Cycle 2 participatory action research project participants were the teachers who volunteered to mentor students at SSHS. Twenty-four teachers submitted notes of interest. The demographics were White females (24%), White males (29%), Black females (8%), and Hispanic females (8%). As the assistant principal, I selected students who need mentoring. Student criteria for participation in the mentoring program involved student grades, attendance, and behavior.

The participatory action research project required that I select individuals to participate in the change initiative. I wanted to ensure the projects success which would result in liberating the minority student from an unjust circumstance. I decided to recruit volunteer mentors.

During this project, I used volunteer mentors as the central group for promoting positive racial teacher-student classroom relationships. Why use teachers who volunteer to mentor students as the central group for promoting positive racial teacher-student classroom relationships? Mentors have unique qualities that can assist me with promoting positive racial teacher-student classroom relationships. Mentoring is a "nurturing process in which a skilled or a more experienced person, serving as a role model, teacher, or sponsor that encourages and counsels a less skilled experienced person for the purpose of promoting the latter's professional and/or personal development" (Anderson & Shannon, 1988, p. 40). Mentors nurture personal growth, educational, and career development between an older individual and a young person that lasts over a period of time and focuses on the younger person's needs (Getzloe, 1997; National Urban League, 1992). Mentors advocate for preadolescents and adolescents by helping young people achieve self-reliance, self-esteem, and improved personal and academic growth (National

Urban League, 1992). Mentoring is an appealing idea to individuals who are looking for ways to better develop youth socially and economically by caring for the youth (Flaxman, 1992). Additionally, Blacks rate teachers high if Blacks consider the teachers mentors (Collier & Powell, 1990). Because of these qualities, I believed mentors were perfect participants for this participatory action research project that focused on promoting positive racial teacher-student classroom relationships.

Mentees will benefit from establishing relationships with the mentors. Thirty-seven percent of the mentees were involved in teacher-student interactions that led to discipline referrals (Sunny Shade High School, 2006). Mentees were involved in 50% of the discipline referrals that resulted in classroom disruptions. Mentees may provide mentors with a valuable resource for promoting positive racial teacher-student classroom relationships.

Consequently, I believed mentors advocated for students who are involved in classroom disruptions. Mentors met with mentees and provided strategies for avoiding conflicts with teachers. I believed mentors were the most obvious persons who have a natural stake in promoting positive racial teacher-student classroom relationships.

Finally, Cycle 3 participants originally included eight teachers. One White male teacher decided not to participate after the second meeting. Teacher gender and ethnic demographics were six White females and one White male. Cycle 3 also included three speakers who were teachers at SSHS, three teachers who I distributed information to, and eight students. Six students volunteered to participate in shared vision development process as a precursor to developing a ninth grade-mentoring program for incoming freshman. The other two students, both Black females, volunteered to participate in process that developed positive teacher-student relationships.

Overview of Action Research Cycles

Cycle 1

Cycle 1's primary focus was to determine the present status of teacher-student classroom relationships at SSHS. After this evaluation, I had the data I needed to develop a future action research process to promote positive racial teacher-student classroom relationships.

Cycle 1 used a concurrent mixed model mixed method research design that has separate research purposes. Each purpose had a data collection and data analysis component. Inferences and a metainference were developed after data collection and data analysis were completed.

Theoretical Framework Purpose

Cycle 1 was the case study pilot project that I conducted for the Leadership Application Fieldwork seminar. I believe a case study provided the best beginning for this research project. Researchers report case studies provide opportunities to evaluate bounded systems. "A bounded system is bounded by time and place" (Cresswell, 1998, p. 61). Case study research provides an in-depth analysis and detailed description of a bounded system (Cresswell, 1998). Case studies provide researchers the opportunity to record espoused theories in use derived from responses that reflect conscious values and beliefs (Osterman & Kottkamp, 2004). The case study research project provided me with information related to classroom disruptions at SSHS.

This case study provided me with the information necessary to develop the change process needed for promoting positive racial teacher-student classroom relationships. Researchers have found that effective teachers promote positive nonverbal (Ikeda & Beebe, 1992; Murray, 1983; Nussbaum, 1992; Ogden, Chappmen, & Doak, 1994; Timmerman, 1995; Weimer, 1990) and verbal behavior (Borich, 1986; Good, 1983; Morganett, 1991; Rosenshine, 1983; Sava, 2002; Wassermann, 1992). Researchers also report student perceptions (Aksoy, 1998; Glasser, 1990; Hamacheck, 1969; Heller, 1996; Heller & Scottile, 1996; Kearney, 1984; Ogden et al., 1994; Papandreou, 1995; Rosenshine, 1983; Shedlin, 1986; Timmerman, 1995; Whitney et al., 2005) and culture (Brown, 1999; Ornstein & Levine, 1990) affect teacher-student classroom relationships. Therefore, I developed the following case study research questions that were used to determine (1) teacher and student verbal and nonverbal behavior, (2) teacher-student cultural differences, and (3) teacher positive relationship development with students in the classroom: The researcher questions are:

1) How do SSHS teachers verbally communicate with students in the classroom?

2) How do SSHS teachers nonverbally communicate with students in the classroom?

3) How do SSHS students verbally communicate with teachers in the classroom?

4) How do SSHS students nonverbally communicate with teachers in the classroom?

5) How do SSHS teachers develop positive teacher-student relationships in the classroom?

6) How do cultural differences between teachers and students influence teacher-student classroom relationships?

Since I planned to pilot the change initiative with a specific representative teacher group, foundational information was pertinent. According to Osterman and Kottkamp (2004) and Senge et al. (2000), pilot groups involved in change initiatives need information. Information gathering was central to the case study focus. "The case study probes deeply and analyzes interactions between factors that explain present status of what influences change or growth" (Best & Kahn, 1998, p. 248).

As one of the assistant principals, I could have demanded that teachers change and grow by ordering the change. However, Bolman and Deal (2003) report top-down change assumes the right idea and legitimate authority will ensure organizational change without considering that midlevel and lower level positions create ways to undermine and overthrow change efforts. You cannot get people to do things by forcing them (Follett, 1926/2001). Ordering teachers would not have helped to solve problems related to the change initiative. Adults see problems as an incompetence indicator and create defenses that prevent problem recognition (Osterman & Kottkamp, 2004). I believed the case study provided information for the change project without compromising future organizational change initiative efforts.

I believed the case study method provided an opportunity to develop trust. Required trust between management and employee increases with initiatives that require people to make personal and systemic change (Senge et al., 1999). If a trust gap develops, then the person advocating the initiative will have credibility reduction, which makes people feel at risk. Leaders build trust by developing credibility with staff (Grazian & Bagin, 1996). People accept the influence of leaders they trust (Kouzes & Posner, 2002). Trust is the key to systemic change (Hall & Hord, 2001). I believed this trust was developed by not exposing case study participant identities. Therefore, case study participants and other teachers were more likely to partake in future change initiatives developed by the researcher such as promoting positive racial teacher-student classroom relationships.

Promoting positive racial teacher-student classroom relationships required determining causes that impeded this objective. Systems thinking is a theoretical framework that can enable me to evaluate present classroom conditions at SSHS regarding teacher-student classroom relationships. Systems thinking is the study of a system's structure and behavior (Senge et al., 2000). Systems' structure and behavior are easy to see when the causes and effects are close enough to see (Bolman & Deal, 2003). However, complex systems have causal and effect loops that are far removed and difficult to analyze (Cyert & March, 1963; Senge, 1990). Senge et al. (2000) recommend analyzing a system by evaluating events, patterns and trends, systemic structure, and mental models. Systems thinking provided me with an assessment process that deciphers information needed to develop change processes that could promote positive racial teacher-student classroom relationships. Therefore, I developed systems thinking research questions (Appendix A).

Data collection.

The data collection process included interviews and document collection. Teachers from various content areas were interviewed in my office during teacher planning and lunch periods. Students were interviewed in my office during the school day. Teachers were required to sign a consent form. Students under 18 years of age were not interviewed without parental permission. Students over 18 years of age were required to sign a consent form. Teachers and students were interviewed for approximately 30 minutes using an interview guide (Appendix B). All interviews were recorded and transcribed. Transcribed interviews were returned to teachers and students to ensure validity by member checking. I collected documents such as student discipline profiles, discipline referrals, student attendance, student failures, and student grades.

Data analysis.

I used qualitative and quantitative processes to analyze documents and interviews. First, qualitative interviews were coded into the following themes: (a) teacher nonverbal communication, (b) teacher verbal communication, (c) student nonverbal communication, (d) student verbal communication, (e) teacher-student relationships, (f) cultural influences, (g) classroom disruptions, and (h) mental models. Second, I used quantitative coding methods to analyze documents such as student discipline profiles, student attendance, student failures, and student grades by using a SSPS software program. The SSPS software program was used to display the following cross tabs: (a) monthly classroom disruptions and student ethnicity, (b) student grade level and the number of incidents, (c) number of incidents and gender, (d) percentage of incidents and ethnicity, (e) ethnicity and percentage of absences, (f) percentage of absences and gender, (g) percentage of absences and student grade level,

(h) tardy percentages and ethnicity, (i) tardy percentages and gender, (j) tardy percentages and grade level, (k) number of Behavioral Development Program (BDP) assignments and grade level, (l) number of BDP assignments and ethnicity, (m) number of BDP assignments and gender, (n) percentage of student grades and gender, (o) percentage of student grades and ethnicity, and (p) percentage of student grades and grade level. The significant Pearson correlations displayed by the SSPS software program were (a) number of absences and BDP assignments, (b) absences and grades, (c) tardiness and grades, and (d) absences and tardiness. Finally, I used qualitative and quantitative analysis to develop responses to the systemic structure analysis guidelines outlined by Senge et al. (2000).

Cycle 1 Leadership Reflection

A narrative report for a case study ends with a reminder that the case study report is one person's encounter with the specific case (Cresswell, 1998). This specific case study involves ethnographic fieldwork. Ethnographic fieldwork includes gathering information through observations, interviews, and document gathering. Ethnographers can focus on personal fieldwork experiences rather than culture and report them as confessional tales that focus on the fieldworker rather than the culture (Maanen, 1988). In an autoethnography, the researcher reports his experiences with a culture and reflects on these experiences (Patton, 2002). Therefore, after completing the case study, I reported cultural experiences and reflections related to the case study as a confessional tale. Confessional tales focus on fieldworker personal biases, character flaws, field experiences, unexpected experiences, emotional biases, new perspectives, shocks and surprises, misconceptions, research limits, others' perceptions of the researcher, researcher behavior, and pros and cons (Maanen, 1988).

I collected case study leadership experiences using a tape recorder to document observations and reflections. I collected documents such as e-mails, memos, and proposals related to the case study. The e-mails and memos are correspondence between the principal, the superintendent, and me. I also met with participants to document any feedback regarding me.

I also used qualitative processes to analyze documents. Documents that I collected enabled me to develop confessional tales. I used coding to analyze digital tape recordings, e-mails, photographs, memos, and proposals into some of the themes outlined by Maanen (1988).

Cycle 2

The primary focus of Cycle 2 was to initialize the participatory action research project by developing an agreed-upon shared vision that promoted positive racial teacher-student classroom relationships. During a structured focus group interview, volunteer mentors and I created the self-identity needed for the participatory action research project by developing personal and shared visions related to promoting positive teacher-student classroom relationships. The Cycle 2 participant action research project used a monostrand mixed method research design that includes data collection and data analysis. A monostrand study includes explanatory or confirmatory research questions that use qualitative or quantitative research methods to answer research questions and make qualitative or quantitative inferences (Tashakkori &

Teddlie, 2003). I composed an inference after the data collection and data analysis processes were completed.

Theoretical Framework Purpose

In Cycle 2, I participated with teachers who volunteered to mentor students to create a self-identity by developing a shared vision that focused on promoting positive teacher-student classroom relationships. Developing self-identity is a necessary component for Cycle 3. The Cycle 3 theoretical framework uses self-reference as a fundamental self-organizing process in which self-identity is a primary component. In addition, shared visions promote a learning focus (Senge, 1990). The research question for Cycle 2 is as follows:

1) What is the shared vision for promoting positive racial teacher-student classroom relationships?

In addition to facilitating the shared vision development process, I provided mentors with new information. Information is required for the next cycle of this participatory action research project. According to Wheatley (1999), self-knowledge requires new information. I developed and presented a PowerPoint presentation that highlighted the salient findings revealed in Cycle 1, and I developed an urban student verbal and nonverbal behavior document (Appendix C). I provided volunteer mentors with information regarding Cycle 1 case study results, the dissertation literature review, and an urban student verbal and nonverbal behavior document (Appendix C). I initialized the self-reference process by providing volunteer mentors with information at this time. After the PowerPoint presentation, I responded to and discussed any questions regarding the information disseminated to them or regarding our mission to promote positive teacher-student classroom relationships. I asked the Cycle 2 participants to develop classroom strategies that promote positive teacher-student classroom relationships and to participate in structured focus group discussions regarding those strategies.

Data collection.

The volunteer mentors and I participated in structured focus group interviews. Structured interviews involve asking respondents the same preestablished questions (Fontana & Frey, 2005). According to Senge

(1990), "Writing a vision statement can be a first step in building shared vision . . ." (p. 213). I prompted volunteer mentors to respond in writing to the following: a) Imagine an occasion when you promoted a positive teacher-student interaction in your classroom. Write down what happened. b) Write your personal vision for promoting positive teacher-student classroom relationships.

Afterwards, I developed a shared vision with all participants by having participants share their personal visions and, as a group, codevelop a shared vision. This shared vision development occurred at the beginning of the school year during the first volunteer mentoring meeting for SSHS students.

Data analysis.

I analyzed the codeveloped shared vision during the developmental process. This occurred during the developmental process to ensure that the shared vision focus was related to promoting positive teacher-student classroom relationships. Having a vision focused on promoting positive teacher-student classroom relationships ensured that the learning focus remained centered on the participatory action research project.

Cycle 2 Leadership Reflection

Cycle 2 leadership was shared vision development. According to Senge et al. (1994), building shared visions begins with (a) telling, (b) selling, (c) testing, (d) consulting, or (e) cocreating. I used the cocreating stage, which involves participants working together to build what they want instead of working together to please the boss (Senge et al., 1994). Cocreation was an important participatory action research component. Since participatory action research is a collaborative social process in which people join together to change practices for better or worse (Kemmis & McTaggert, 2005), I used the cocreation process. I answered the self-reflective questions, which correspond to the cocreation stage (Appendix D) outlined by Senge et al. (1994). Self-reflection is also an important participatory action research component. Participatory action researchers reflect to understand their practices as they emerge within their own social circumstances (Kemmis & McTaggert, 2005).

I responded to cocreating the shared vision questions immediately after the meeting by creating field notes. I also used a tape recorder to record any data necessary to respond to the questions for cocreating a shared vision. I coded my field notes and transcriptions into a narrative format that answers the Cycle 2 leadership questions. The narrative format described the setting and included responses related to the cocreation shared vision development outlined by Senge et al. (1999). I reported team participation in Cycle 2 as a confessional tale, too. Confessional tales focus on the fieldworker rather than on the culture (Maanen, 1988). Confessional tales focus on fieldworker personal biases, character flaws, field experiences, unexpected experiences, emotional biases, new perspectives, shocks and surprises, misconceptions, research limits, others' perceptions of the researcher, researcher behavior, and pros and cons (Maanen, 1988).

Cycle 3

I am a Black assistant principal in a school that has 93% White teaching staff, 67% White administrative staff, 99% Black and Hispanic student population, and 99% of the students qualified for reduced or free lunch. These racial, power, and socioeconomic dynamics can provide a disadvantage for students and me when attempting a diversity initiative that involves promoting positive racial teacher-student classroom relationships.

Racial dynamics can cause cultural and power-related conflicts between the staff and me. According to Bolman and Deal (2003), poor management related to cultural conflicts can lead to infighting and a destructive power struggle. I believed if I took an approach that required teachers to submit to my demands, then teachers would have become defensive and develop characteristics consistent with organizational malaise and defensive routines that are counterproductive to the participatory action research project success. I believed by implementing self-knowledge, as suggested by Wheatley (1999), change could take place without defensive routines that embarrass or threaten teachers. Self-knowledge enables organizational change by self-organization that correlates to a self-reference point (Wheatley, 1999). Using self-knowledge also focused on problem solving by empowering teachers, which consequently empowers students, and did not focus on race even though race incompatibilities between teachers and students are the real issue.

Conflicts between staff and students can result from racial dynamics. Researchers report that these racial dynamics can present difficulties for marginalized students. Discrimination against marginalized students is a persistent problem in classrooms throughout the United States (Garcia, 1984). White female teachers interact with White students better than Black students (Byalick & Bershoff, 1974). A teacher's economic class level has greater negative influence on Black students when compared to White students (Alexander, Entwisle, & Thompson, 1987). Classroom interaction studies have found teachers discriminate against students who are not White, male, and middle class (Entwise & Webster, 1974; Safilios-Rothchild, 1979). Ogbu (1987) reports that students believe school is detrimental to their identity when they are incorporated into a society by slavery, conquest, or colonization. Students who attend SSHS may have developed these values as a tradition from their parents. The racial dynamics can cause low student achievement and discipline challenges for students at SSHS. Since the challenge was to implement a change model that minimizes conflict among teachers, students, and me, I used Wheatley's self-knowledge model for Cycle 3.

The research design for Cycle 3 was a concurrent mixed model mixed method that had separate research purposes. Each purpose had a data type and data analysis. I developed inferences and metainferences after data collection and data analysis were completed.

Theoretical Framework Purpose

I used the self-knowledge change model concept suggested by Wheatley as a change model for Cycle 3 due to the racial dynamics involved in this change project. According to Wheatley (1999), a system changes when it learns more about itself by implementing processes that facilitate self-discovery and create new relationships. Figure 3 reveals the self-knowledge paradigm. Wheatley (1999) stated:

> My colleagues and I focus on helping a system
> develop greater self-knowledge in three critical
> areas. People need to be connected to the
> fundamental identity of the organization or

community. Who are we? Who do we aspire to become? How shall we be together? Moreover, people need to be connected to new information. What else do we need to know? Where is this new information to be found? In addition, people need to be able to reach past traditional boundaries and develop relationships with people anywhere in the system. Who else needs to be here to do this work with us? (p. 146)

The research questions for this self-knowledge theoretical framework are as follows:

1) What information do teachers need to promote positive racial teacher-student classroom relationships?

2) With whom do teachers, to promote positive racial teacher-student classroom relationships, need to develop relationships?

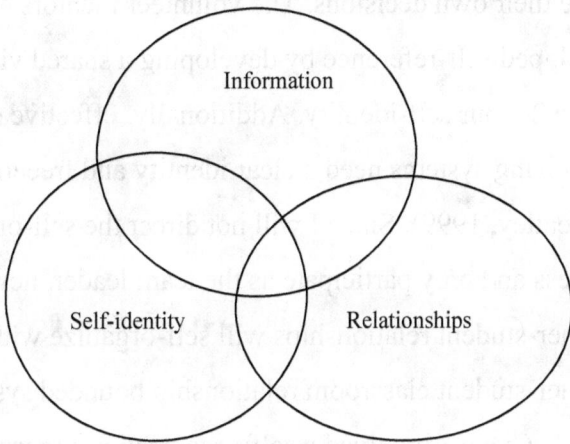

Figure 3 Self-knowledge theoretical framework.

I believed teacher-student classroom relationships redeveloped because they implemented an agreed-upon self-identity and new information that I provided. According to Wheatley (1999), self-organizing systems change to preserve their self-reference point. Without self-reference, the system has no predetermined course. Self-reference is a self-organizational process by which when a system shifts and needs to change it will change in such a manner that it remains consistent with itself. Effective self-organization includes guidance by a clear organizational identity for people to reference and freedom for people to make their own decisions. The volunteer mentors and I developed self-reference by developing a shared vision in Cycle 2—our self-identity. Additionally, effective self-organizing systems need a clear identity and freedom (Wheatley, 1999). Since I will not direct the self-organizing process and only participate as the team leader, new teacher-student relationships will self-organize within the teacher-student classroom relationship bounded system.

Cycle 3 involved a self-organization process in which students, teachers, and I, at SSHS, became involved to promote positive racial teacher-student classroom relationships. Wheatley (1999) stated:

> The viability and resiliency of a self-organizing system comes from its great capacity to adapt as needed, to create structures that fit the moment. Neither form nor function alone dictates how the system is organized. Instead, they are process structures, reorganizing into different forms in order to maintain itself in its present form or evolve to a new order depending on what is required. It is not locked into any one structure; it is capable of

> organizing into what form it determines best suits
> the present situation. (p. 82)

Therefore, I was not able to predict my role, the teachers' roles, or the students' roles in Cycle 3.

The new relationship developments need an assessment process. Senge et al. (1999) report that skeptics will want to know how to prove any new training efforts. In this case, skeptics will want to know how I can prove my efforts promoted positive racial teacher-student classroom relationships. Senge et al. (1999) recommend (a) tracking the number of new innovations within the pilot group, (b) looking at observable behavior indicators to measure project impact, and (c) evaluating pilot group influence on the organization. Therefore, I used the following explanatory research questions to prove that my efforts promoted positive racial teacher-student classroom relationships at SSHS:

1) What new innovations were developed that promote positive racial teacher-student classroom relationships?

2) What observable data indicate the impact of promoting positive racial teacher-student classroom relationships?

3) How have participating teachers promoting positive racial teacher-student classroom relationships influenced SSHS?

Data collection.

I collected qualitative data by completing classroom observations and conducting structured focus group interviews using a digital journal. During the structured focus group interviews, the project participants and I discussed newly developed strategies that promote positive teacher-student classroom relationships. I also conducted student focus group interviews. I used reflective practice during the student focus group interviews. Reflective practice is a form of professional development that changes assumptions about learning and behavior (Osterman & Kottkamp, 2004). I decided to use the left-hand column activity originally developed by Argyris and Schon (1974). I developed a left-hand column activity, which I distributed to students during our meeting (Appendix Q).

Data analysis.

I used qualitative processes to analyze documents. I also analyzed focus group discussions and digital recordings by coding. Coded themes included school discipline and student achievement.

Cycle 3 Leadership Reflection

Cycle 3 leadership includes participative management. Participative management is a new science leadership component outlined by Wheatley (1999). Participative management involves empowering employees to participate in the decision-making process with their supervisors (Argyris, 1955). Participative management involves power sharing between the team leader and team members (Anthony, 1978; Sashkin, 1982; Williams, 1976). Participative management team leaders lead with the best interest for themselves, the team members, and the organization (Anthony, 1978). I reported team leader participation in Cycle 3 as participative management outlined by Wheatley (1999). According to Wheatley (1999), participative management focuses on relationships, seen and unseen, information sharing and deciphering, self-organization, and self-reference. Wheatley (1999) stated:

> I believe in my bones that the movement towards participation is rooted in our changing perceptions of the organizing principals of life. Everywhere in the new sciences, in living systems theory, quantum physics, chaos and complexity theory, we observe life's dependence on participation. All life participates in the current creation of itself, insisting on the freedom to self-determine. All life participates actively with its environment in the process of co-adaptation and co-evolution…. That has required scientist to focus their attention on relationships. No one can contemplate a system's view of life without becoming engrossed in relational dynamics. (p. 163)

Additionally, Wheatley (1999) stated, "Participation and relationships are only two of our present dilemmas" (p. 165). "If we fail to recognize information's essential role in supporting self-organization, we will be unable to survive in this new world" (p. 166).

I collected Cycle 3 leadership experiences using a tape recorder to document observations and reflections, which revealed participative management leadership and any other leadership characteristics that evolved. I collected documents such as e-mails and memos related to Cycle 3 leadership participation.

Cycle 4

In the previous cycles, I studied my leadership by using reflection processes that were specific to the participatory action research change cycle. In Cycle 1, I used confessional tales to report my leadership. In Cycle 2, I reported my participation as a cocreator of the shared vision. According to Senge et al. (1994), building shared visions begins with (a) telling, (b) selling, (c) testing, (d) consulting, or (e) cocreating. I used the cocreating stage, which involved action research participants and me working together to build what we wanted instead of working together to please the boss. In Cycle 3, I reported my leadership from the participative management perspective. In Cycle 4, I reported my leadership from three other perspectives. The first perspective was reflective questions that triangulated my leadership, as outlined by Patton (2002). The second perspective was the correlation between leadership characteristics outlined by Kouzes and Posner (2002) and specific components of my leadership platform. The third perspective was my ethical decision-making process that I outlined in the leadership platform.

The research design for Cycle 4 is concurrent mixed model mixed method. Autoethnography, Likert scale survey, participant action research cycle leadership reflections, and digital journal reflections are the quantitative and qualitative research methods that I used to report the leadership participation aspects of the research project. The research questions are qualitative, and the theoretical Likert scale questions are quantitative. I analyzed both sets of data types, wrote separate inferences, and developed a metainference that combines all leadership data collection and reflections for this cycle.

Theoretical Framework Purpose

Researchers report an autoethnography creates controversies among qualitative theorists (Patton, 2002). Crotty (1998) reports autoethnographies are rampant literary writings. According to Patton (2002), "Many social science academics object to the way [autoethnographies] blur the lines between social science and literary writing" (p. 86). To ensure autoethnography quality, Patton (2002) recommends responding to reflective questions that triangulate inquiry. Therefore, I responded to reflective questions that triangulated autoethnography inquiry (Appendix E).

I also used the leadership challenge (LC) to report leadership for this participatory action research project. The LC components include (a) model the way, (b) inspire a shared vision, (c) challenge the process, (d) enable others to act, and (e) encourage the heart. Each LC component corresponds to elements in my leadership platform. The model the way component includes personal mastery, which is a component of my leadership platform. Personal mastery development originates through personal vision reflection (Senge et al., 2000), which can include leadership beliefs and values analysis. According to Kouzes and Posner (2002), credible leaders model the way by demonstrating a commitment to beliefs that result from value clarification and self-expression. Credible leaders fully comprehend their values, beliefs, and assumptions before communicating leadership objectives. The inspire a shared vision LC component includes shared vision development, team formulation, persuasion skills, and planning skills elements that are integrated in my leadership platform. Shared vision development requires leaders to enlist others by cocreating organizational strategies to enhance productivity (Senge et al., 1994). According to Kouzes and Posner (2002), leaders enlist others in shared visions by finding and focusing on common organizational objectives instead of imposing their vision on others. The challenging the process LC component includes problem-solving skills, using pilot groups, and risk-taking skills that are included in my leadership platform. Kouzes and Posner (2002) report that effective leaders challenge processes by using pilot groups and taking risks to solve organizational problems. The enabling others to act LC component includes building cultural linkages, empowering others, and creating collaborative group development elements, which are included in my leadership platform. Effective leaders enable others to act by fostering collaborative goals that promote and build trust and share power with others (Kouzes & Posner, 2002). The encouraging the heart LC component requires leaders to recognize and celebrate others' contributions by focusing on clear standards. Focusing on clear standards requires leaders to set goals, which is also a component of my leadership platform.

Data collection.

I used a digital tape recorder to record cultural experiences. I then transcribed the recorded cultural experiences and reflections into field notes. I also used a Kouzes and Posner (2002) Leadership Practices Inventory (LPI). The LPI is an instrument that provides feedback regarding leadership behavior and includes a self and observer survey. I completed a 30-item self-assessment of the five components related to the leadership challenge. Teachers and staff members completed a 30-item leader observer assessment. Finally, I responded to questions that parallel the five leadership challenge components (Appendix J).

Data analysis.

I analyzed transcribed recordings and responded to research questions that triangulated the autoethnography inquiry. According to Patton (2002), autoethnography analysis includes (a) self-reflexivity, (b) reflexivity about those studied, and (c) reflectivity about the audience (Appendix F). I administered an LPI survey.

REFERENCES

Aksoy, N. (1998). Opinions of Upper Elementary Students About a "Good Teacher" Case Study in turkey. *ED428042.*

Alexander, K., Entwisle, D., & Thompson, M. (1987). School performance, status relations, and the structure of sentiment: Bringing the teacher back in. *American Sociological Review, 52(5)*, 665-682.

Anderson, E., & Shannon, A. (1988). Toward a Conceptualization of Mentoring. *Journal of Teacher Education, 39*(1), 38-42.

Anthony, W. (1984). *Participative Management.* Reading, Massachusetts: Addison-Wesley.

Argyris, C. (1955). Organizational Leadership and Participative Management. *The Journal of Business, 28*(1), 1-7.

Argyris, C. (1990). *Overcoming Organizational Defenses: Facilitating Organizational Change.* Upper Saddle River, NJ: Prentice Hall.

Argyris, C., & Schon, D. (1974). *Theory in Practice: Increasing professional effectiveness.* Boston: Allyn and Bacon.

Bennett, C. (1997). Teaching students as they would be taught: The importance of cultural perspective. In B. Shade (Ed.), *Culture, Style, and the Educative Process: Making Schools Work for Racially Diverse Students* (2nd, pp. 129-142). Springfield, Ill.: Charles C. Thomas.

Berg, B. (2007). *Qualitative Research Methods for the Social Sciences* (6th). Boston: Pearson.

Best, J., & Kahn, J. (1998). *Research in Education* (8th). Needham Heights, MA: A Viacom Company.

Bolman, L., & Deal, T. (2003). *Reframing Organizations: Artistry, Choice, and Leadership.* San Francisco: Jossey-Bass.

Borich, G. (1986). Paradigm of teacher effectiveness research? Their relationship to the concept of effective teaching. *Education and Urban Society, 13(18)*, 143-167.

Boykin, A. (1979). Psychological/behavioral verve: Some theoretical explorations and empirical manifestations. In A. Boykin, A. Franklin & J. Yates (Eds.), *Research Directions of Black Psychologists.* New York: Russel Sage Foundation.

Brown, D. (1999). Proven Strategies for Improving Learning & Achievement. *ED430179.*

Byalick, R., & Bershoff, D. (1974). Reinforcement practices of black and white teachers in integrated classrooms. *Journal of Educational Psychology, 66*(4), 473-480.

Campbell, D., & Fiske, D. (1959). Convergent and Discriminant Validation by Multitrait-multimethod Matrix. *Psychological Bulletin, 56(2)*, 81-105.

Chappell, C., & McCoy, L. (2003). Studies in Teaching. In Wake Forest University (Ed.), *Research Digest: Research Projects Presented at Annual Research Forum.* Winston-Salem, NC: Wake Forest University.

Collier, J., & Powell, R. (1990). Ethnicity, Instructional Communication and Classroom Systems. *Communication Quarterly, 38*(4), 334-349.

Cresswell, J. (1998). *Qualitative inquiry and research design: Choosing among five traditions.* Thousand Oaks, CA: Sage.

Cresswell, J. (2003). *Research Design: Qualitative, Quantitative, and Mixed Methods Approaches* (2nd). Thousand Oaks, CA: Sage Publications.

Crotty, M. (1998). *The Foundations of Social Research: Meaning and Perspective in the Research Process.* Thousand Oaks: Sage Publications.

Cyert, R., & March, J. (1963). *A Behavioral Theory of the Firm.* Englewood Cliffs, NJ: Prentice Hall.

Edmonds, H. (2000). *The Focus Group Research Handbook.* Thousand Oaks, CA: Sage Publications.

Entwise, D., & Webster, M. (1974). Expectations in Mixed Racial Groups. *Sociology of Education, 47*, 301-318.

Flaxman, E. (1992). The Mentoring Relationship in Action. *ED356287.*

Follett, M. (2001). The Giving of Orders. In D. Tatom (Ed.), *Classics of Organizational Theory.* Belmont CA: Wadsworth. (Original work published 1926)

Fontana, A., & Frey, J. (2005). The Interview: From Neutral Stance to Political Involvement. In N. Denzin & Y. Lincoln (Eds.), *The Sage Handbook of Qualitative Research* (3rd). Thousand Oaks, CA: Sage Publications.

Garcia, R. (1984). Countering Classroom Discrimination. *Theory into Practice, 23*(2), 104-109.

Gates, D. (1998). Diversity Issues in Teaching: Cultural Sensitivity in the Classroom. *ED425482.*

Gay, G. (1975). Cultural Differences Important in Education of Black Children. *Momentum,* 30-31.

Gay, G. (1975). Teachers' achievement expectations of and classroom interactions with ethnically different students. *Contemporary Education, 46(3)*, 166-172.

Getzloe, E. (1997). The power of positive relationships: Mentoring programs in the school and community. *Preventing School Failure, 41(3)*, 100-104.

Gilbert, S., & Gay, G. (1985). Improving the Success in School of Poor Black Children. *Phi Delta Kappan, 67*(2), 133-137.

Glasser, W. (1990). *The Quality School: Managing students without coercion* (1st). New York: Harper and Row.

Glense, C. (2006). *Becoming Qualitative Researchers: An Introduction* (3rd). Boston: Pearson Education, Inc.

Good, T. (1983). Classroom research: A decade of progress. *Educational Psychologist, 18(3)*, 127-144.

Good, T., & Brophy, J. (1972). Behavioral expression of teacher attitudes. *Journal of Educational Psychology, 63(6)*, 617-624.

Hall, G., & Hord, S. (2001). *Implementing Change: Patterns, Principles, and Potholes.* Boston: Allyn and Bacon.

Hamacheck, D. (1969). Characteristics of good teachers and implications for teacher education. *Phi Delta Kappan, 50(6),* 341-344.

Heller, D. (1996). Another Look at Student Motivation. *ED398524.*

Heller, D., & Scottile, J. (1996). Another Look at Student Motivation: A qualitative study. *ED398524.*

Holstein, J., & Gubruim, J. (2005). Interpretive Practice and Social Action. In N. Denzin & Y. Lincoln (Eds.), *The Sage Handbook of Qualitative Research* (3rd). Thousand Oaks, CA: Sage Publications.

Hurlock, E. (1924). The Value of Praise and Reproof as Incentives for Children. *Archeology Psychology, 71,* 1-78.

Ikeda, T., & Beebe, S. (1992). A Review of Teacher Nonverbal Immediacy: Implications for Intercultural Research. *ED349592.*

Kamberelis, G., & Dimitriadis, G. (2005). Focus Groups: Strategic Articulations of Pedagogy, Politics, and Inquiry. In N. Denzin & Y. Lincoln (Eds.), *The Sage Handbook of Qualitative Research* (3rd). Thousand Oaks, CA: Sage Publications.

Kearney, P. (1984). Perceptual discrepancies in teacher communication style. *Communication Education, 13,* 95-108.

Keith, T., Tornatzky, L., & Pettigrew, L. (1974). An Analysis of Verbal and Nonverbal Classroom Teaching Behaviors. *The Journal of Experimental Education, 42*(4), 30-38.

Kouzes, J., & Posner, B. (2002). *The Leadership Challenge.* San Francisco, CA: Jossey-Bass.

Maanen, V. (1988). *Tales of the field: On writing ethnography.* Chicago: University of Chicago Press.

Meridith, E. (2000). *Leadership Strategies for Teachers.* Arlington Heights, IL: Skylight Professional Development.

Mertens, D. (2003). Mixed Methods and the politics of human research: The transformative-emancipatory perspective. In A. Tashakkori & C. Teddlie (Eds.), *Handbook of Mixed Methods in the Social Sciences and Behavioral Sciences.* Thousand Oaks, CA: Sage Publications.

Milburn, T. (2000). Inferring Cultural Learning Styles - Puerto Ricans in the US. *ED448492.*

Moghaddam, F., Walker, B., & Harre', R. (2003). Cultural Distance, Levels of Abstraction, and the

Advantages of Mixed Methods. In A. Tashakkori & C. Teddlie (Eds.), *Handbook of Mixed Methods in Social & Behavioral Research.* Thousand Oaks, CA: Sage Publications.

Morganett, L. (1991). Good teacher-student relationships: A key element for classroom motivation and management. *Education, 112(2)*, 260-264.

Murray, H. (1983). Low-Inference Classroom Teaching Behaviors and Student Ratings of College Teaching Effectiveness. *Journal of Educational Psychology, 75(1)*, 138-149.

National Urban League. (1992). Mentoring Young Black Males: An Overview. *ED377290.*

Nussbaum, J. (1992). Effective Teacher Behaviors. *Communication Education, 41(2)*, 167-180.

Ogbu, J. (1987). Variability in Minority School Performance: A Problem in Search of an Explanation. *Anthropology and Education Quarterly, 18(4)*, 312-334.

Ogbu, J. (1992). Adaptation to Minority Status and Impact on School Success. *Theory Into Practice, 31*(4), 287-295.

Ogbu, J. (1992). Understanding Cultural Diversity and Learning. *Educational Researcher, 21*(8), 5-14 + 24.

Ogden, D., Chappmen, A., & Doak, L. (1994). Characteristics of Good/Effective Teachers: Gender Differences in Student Descriptors. *ED383657.*

Ornstein, A., & Levine, D. (1990). Class, Race, and Achievement. *Education Digest, 55*(9), 11-14.

Osterman, K., & Kottkamp, R. (2004). *Reflective Practice for Educators: Professional Development to Improve Student Learning.* Thousand Oaks, CA: Corwin Press.

Papandreou, A. (1995). Teaching Viewed Through Student Performance and Selected Effectiveness Factors. *ED392760.*

Rosenshine, B. (1983). Teaching Functions in Instructional Programs. *The Elementary School Journal, 83(4),* 335-351.

Safilios-Rothchild, C. (1979). *Sex-role socialization and sex discrimination: A synthesis and critique of the literature.* Washington, DC: National Institute of Education.

Sashkin, M. (1982). *A Manger's Guide to Participative Management.* USA: AMA Membership Publications Division.

Sava, F. (2002). Causes and effects of teacher conflict-inducing attitudes towards pupils: a path analysis model. *Teaching and Teacher Education, 18(8),* 1007-1021.

Senge, P. (1990). *The Fifth Discipline: The Art and Practice of the Learning Organization.* New York: Doubleday.

Senge, P., Cambron-McCabe, N., Lucas, T., Smith, B., Dutton, J., & Kliener, A. (2000). *Schools that Learn: A Fifth Discipline Fieldbook for Educators, Parents, and Everyone Who Cares about Education.* New York: Doubleday.

Senge, P., Kleiner, A., Roberts, C., Ross, R., Roth, G., & Smith, B. (1999). *The Dance of Change: The Challenges of Sustaining Momentum in Learning Organizations.* New York: Doubleday.

Senge, P., Kliener, A., Roberts, C., Ross, R., & Smith, B. (1994). *The Fifth Discipline Fieldbook: Strategies and Tools for Building a Learning Organization.* New York: Doubleday.

Shade, B. (1997). The Culture and Style of Mexican-American Society. In B. Shade (Ed.), *Culture, Style, and the Educative Process: Making Schools Work for Racially Diverse Students.* Springfield, Ill: Charles C. Thomas.

Shade, B. (1997). African-American Cognitive Patterns: A review of the Research. In B. Shade (Ed.), *Culture, Style, and the Educative Process: Making Schools Work for Racially Diverse Students.* Springfield, Ill.: Charles C. Thomas.

Shade, B. (1997). Culture and Learning Style within the African-American Community. In B. Shade (Ed.), *Culture, Style, and the Educative Process: Making Schools Work for Racially Diverse Students.* Springfield, Ill.: Charles C. Thomas.

Shade, B. (1997). Culture: The Key to Adaptation. In B. Shade (Ed.), *Culture, Style and the Educative Process: Making Schools Work for Racially Diverse Students.* Springfield, Ill.: Charles C. Thomas.

Shade, B. (1997). Teaching to an African-American Cognitive Style. In B. Shade (Ed.), *Culture, Style and the Educative Process: Making schools work for racially diverse students.* Springfield, ILL.: Charles C. Thomas.

Shade, B., Kelly, C., & Oberg, M. (1997). *Creating Culturally Responsive Classroom* (1st). Washington, DC: American Psychological Association.

Shedlin, A. (1986). 487 sixth graders can't be wrong. *Principal, 66(1)*, 53.

Tashakkori, A., & Teddlie, C. (Eds.). (2003). *Handbook of Mixed Methods in Social & Behavioral Research.* Thousand Oaks, CA: Sage Publications.

Timmerman, L. (1995). Rhetorical Dimensions of Teaching Effectiveness. *ED386761.*

Wassermann, S. (1992). Asking the Right Question: The Essence of Teacher Fastback 343. *ED355234.*

Weimer, M. (1990). *Improving college teaching: Strategies for developing instructional effectiveness* (1st). San Francisco: Jossey Bass.

Weiss, R. (1994). *Learning From Strangers: The Art and Method of Qualitative Interview Studies.* New York: The Free Press.

Wheatley, M. (1999). *Leadership and the New Science: Discovering Order in a Chaotic World* (2nd). San Francisco: Berrett-Koehler.

Whitney, J., Leonard, M., Leonard, W., Camelio, M., & Camelio, V. (2005). Seek balance, connect with others, and reach all students: High school students describe a moral imperative for teachers. *High School Journal, 89*(2), 29-38.

Williams, E. (1976). *Participative Management: Concepts, Theory and Implementation.* Atlanta, GA: Georgia State University.

Appendix A

<u>Case Study Systemic Evaluation Questions</u>

The questions related to evaluating events are:

1) What is a classroom/shop disruption?

2) How have teachers and students responded to classroom/shop disruptions?

3) How have teachers and students tried to solve class/shop disruptions?

The questions related to patterns and trends are:

1) What is the history of classroom/shop disruptions?

2) When do classroom/shop disruptions occur?

3) After charting classroom/shop disruptions over time, what patterns emerge?

The questions related to systemic structure are:

1) What forces create classroom/shop disruptions?

2) How do these systemic elements seem to influence each other?

3) What fundamental aspects of the school must

    change, if you want to change the patterns?

The questions related to mental models are:

1) What is it about the teachers thinking that causes

    classroom/shop disruptions?

2) What is it about the students thinking that causes

    classroom/shop disruptions?

Appendix B

Case Study Interview Guide

The questions formulated for the teacher interview guide are:

1) Describe an incident that resulted in a classroom/shop disruption.

2) How did the classroom/shop disruption incident make you feel? Why?

3) How did you handle the classroom/shop disruption?

4) What conclusions do have about the classroom/shop disruptions?

5) Is there anything you or the student could have done to avoid the classroom/shop disruption?

6) How do you verbally communicate with students in the classroom?

7) How do you non-verbally communicate with students in the classroom?

8) How do you develop positive teacher-student relationships in the classroom?

9) How do you consider students culture when developing positive teacher-student relationships in the classroom?

Questions formulated for the student interview guide are:

1) Describe an incident that resulted in a classroom/shop disruption.

2) How did the classroom/shop disruption incident make you feel? Why?

3) How did you handle the classroom/shop disruption?

4) What conclusions do have about the classroom/shop disruptions?

5) Is there anything you or the teacher could have done to avoid the classroom/shop disruption?

6) How do you verbally communicate with teachers in the classroom?

7) How do you non-verbally communicate with teachers in the classroom?

8) How do you develop student-teacher relationships in the classroom?

How do you consider the teachers culture when developing student-teacher relationships in the classroom?

Appendix C

Urban Student Verbal, nonverbal, and Classroom Behavior

Nonverbal

- [Some urban students] either nod their head or verbally respond to indicate that they are listening to the speaker (Erickson, 1979; Feldman, 2001).

- [Some urban students] are better able to recognize faces and emotions than other ethnic groups (Chance, Goldstein, & McBride, 1975; Galper, 1973; Gitter, Black, & Mostofsky, 1972), and are extremely sensitive to social situation nuances (Hill & Fox, 1973; Witmer & Ferinden, 1970).

- [Some urban Students] have a high sensitivity to facial expressions (Shade, Kelly, & Oberg, 1997).

- When [some urban students] sense hostility and nonacceptance they assess the circumstance through nonverbal cues (Shade et al., 1997).

- [Some urban students] have a highly "developed skill to understand and correctly perceive the affective dimensions of people and situations" (Shade et al., 1997, p. 26).

Verbal

- [Some urban students] use jokes and humor to avoid verbal disagreements because diplomacy and tact are valued communication skills (Shade, 1997).

- [Some urban] children are inclined to talk back when motivated by what a teacher says (Gay, 1975).

- [Some urban] students will argue for recognition of unsuccessful efforts towards completing a task (Gilbert & Gay, 1985).

- [Some urban] children are socialized to say one thing and do another (Gay, 1975).

- When [Urban] "children are motivated by what their teachers have to say, their inclination is to talk back" (Gay, 1975, p. 32).

- [Some urban students] verbally respond to indicate that they are listening to the speaker (Erickson, 1979).

- [Some urban students] indicate they are listening by making short sounds (Feldman, 2001).

- [Some urban students] verbally communicate by telling the truth or telling it like it is (Shade et al., 1997).

- [Some urban students] communities view truth telling or telling it like it is verbal communication as courageous, honest, and refusing to compromise integrity (Shade et al., 1997).

- [Some urban students] use jokes and humor to verbally communicate (Shade et al., 1997).

- [Some urban] students are taught to project their personalities and call attention to their individual talents while involved in play (Gay, 1975).

- [Some urban students] use indirectas, a form of speech that is an indirect way of making something known (Milburn, 2000). "Indirectas are literally, indirect statements critical of others – insinuations, innuendo. They are disguised or purposely vague to any but the initiated, but clear in meaning to the ones who know the circumstance or the people involved. In form they do not give away either the person speaking or the person spoken of; they seem not to be barbed and directed to particulars, but they are meaningful in context. Anyone who is "in the know" does know how they are to be applied" (Morris, 1981, p. 102).

- [Some urban students] manifest modal personality traits such as tendency toward orderliness (Martinez, 1977).

- [Some urban students] prefer a socially interactive environment (Slavin, 1983).

Classroom

- Dividing learning activities into segments by days may hinder or be less meaningful to [some urban] students (Milburn, 2000).

- [Some urban] children prefer to work with an authority figure rather than work alone (Sierra, 1973).

- [Some urban] achievers have the ability to induce negative reactions from their teachers (Shade, 1978).

- [Some urban] gifted achievers receive less attention, are least praised, and most criticized in a classroom, when compared to non-achieving and non-gifted counterparts (Rubovits & Maehr, 1973).

- Some urban students work better in a classroom environment that is cooperative, informal, and loosely structured (Gilbert & Gay, 1985).

- [Some urban] students work better in a classroom "where students and teachers work closely together to achieve common goals" (Gilbert & Gay, 1985, p. 134).

- [Some urban] "Children will work together to benefit the group" (Gilbert & Gay, 1985, p. 134).

- [Some urban] children are socialized to use metaphors and symbolism to approach issues in a round about manner (Gay, 1975).

- [Some urban] "Child's involvement in cognitive classroom activities is likely to be signaled by vocal responses, exuberance, and physical movement" (Gay, 1975, p. 32).

- Before [some urban] students begin a task they may look over the assignment in its

86

entirety, rearrange posture and writing space, ask the teacher to repeat the directions, check the perception of other neighboring students, and check pencils and paper. For [some urban] students these are necessary classroom behaviors while teachers may perceive that the students are inattentive, disruptive, not prepared, or attempting to avoid completing the task (Gilbert & Gay, 1985).

- [Some urban students] are proficient at gathering, using, and analyzing kinesthetic information (Shade, 1997).

- [Some urban students] prefer affective materials to facilitate their learning (Rychlak, 1975), warm and supportive teachers (St. John, 1971), and a socially interactive environment (Cureton, 1978; Slavin, 1983).

- [Some urban students] have a low tolerance for monotonous or low-level activity and prefer and need a constant change of information coupled with a variety of information (Boykin, 1979).

- [Some urban students] sorting behavior includes a top-down approach instead of a bottom-up approach which is utilized by most teachers (Shade, 1997).

- [Some urban students] do well on tasks that require auditory sensory involvement but have challenges when tasks require visual perception (Guinagh, 1971; Hall & Kaye, 1977).

- [Some urban students] may seek peer assistance as much as teacher assistance (Gay & Abrahams, 1976).

- [Some urban students] are taught that question and answer sessions result when an adult is angry with them and this process may inhibit students from classroom involvement (Bennett, 1997).

- "When [some urban] students are forced to separate only the cognitive component for use in the classroom, they feel that this is unnatural and find it difficult to honor the teacher's request" (Gilbert & Gay, 1985, p. 135).

- Orderly classroom environments are dull, stagnant, and unstimulating to [some urban] students (Gilbert & Gay, 1985).

- [Some urban] students demonstrate the ability to teach and learn simultaneously in an informal environment amongst their peers (Gay, 1975).

- [Some urban] children learn at an early age to combine words with a dynamic interplay of body movements, intonations, and gestures (Gay, 1975).

- [Some urban] students in mainstream classrooms address and respond to teachers clearly, concisely, and require that the teacher look at them. In bilingual classrooms [some urban] may lower their heads, look away, and giggle (Ortiz, 1988).

- [Some urban students] make decisions jointly where one person speaks and others join in and respond until a decision is made (Milburn, 2000).

- [Some urban students] involved in the decision-making processes may use rising intonation, qualifies, questions, and hedges (Milburn, 2000).

- [Some urban students] value group relationships and consensus decision-making (Milburn, 2000).

- [Some urban students] value people and relationships over task accomplishment (Morales-Jones, 1998).

- [Some urban students] are comfortable with attending to more than one task at a time (Morales-Jones, 1998).

- Some mainstreamed [urban] students were unwilling to ask guest speakers questions (McClure, 1978).

- When teachers require only cognitive activities, [some urban] students feel that the request is unnatural and have difficulty following the teacher's request that results in frustration and withdrawal for [some urban] students (Gay, 1975).

- [Some urban students] prefer a greater social distance when compared to [other urban students] (Shade, 1997).

- [Some urban students] modes of perception are more auditory and tactile than visual and literate (Keil, 1966).

- [Some urban students] categorize pictorial representations in a more relational or holistic manner rather than an analytical or detailed oriented manner (Sigel, Anderson, & Shapiro, 1966).

- [Some urban students] sort word list by their functional value (Orasanu, Lee, & Scribner, 1979).

- [Some urban] children attempt to learn collectively and maximize their intellectual exchange and knowledge acquisition by working together on assignments that may result in [some urban] students copying answers from each other (Shade, 1997).

Miscellaneous

- [Some urban students] are willing to conform to classroom rules to attempt to overcome difficulties in school because crossing cultural lines is an advantage to survival (Ogbu, 1992).

- Immigrant [urban] students are moderately motivated and well behaved (Patthey-Chavez, 1993).

- [Some urban students] are not willing to perform well in school due to difficulty in crossing cultural lines (Ogbu, 1992).

- [Some urban] children are socialized to achieve direction through indirection. Their speech and behavior often appear contradictory because they seem to say one thing and mean and/or do another" (Gay, 1975, p. 32).

References

Bennett, C. (1997). Teaching students as they would be taught: The importance of cultural perspective. In B. Shade (Ed.), *Culture, Style, and the Educative Process: Making Schools Work for Racially Diverse Students.* Springfield, Ill.: Charles C. Thomas.

Boykin, A. (1979). Psychological/behavioral verve: Some theoretical explorations and empirical manifestations. In A. Boykin, A. Franklin & J. Yates (Eds.), *Research Directions of Black Psychologists.* New York: Russell Sage Foundation.

Chance, J., Goldstein, A., & McBride, L. (1975). Differential experience and recognition memory for faces. *Journal of Social Psychology, 97*, 243-253.

Cureton, G. (1978). Using a black learning style. *The Reading Teacher, 1*, 751-756.

Erickson, F. (1979). Talking down: Some cultural sources of miscommunication in interracial interviews.

Nonverbal behavior: Applications and cross-cultural implications. New York: Academic Press.

Feldman, R. (2001). Nonverbal Behavior, Race, and the Classroom. *Teacher Theory and Practice, 24*(1), 45-49.

Galper, R. (1973). Functional race membership and recognition of faces. *Perceptual and Motor Skills, 37*, 455-462.

Gay, G. (1975). Cultural Differences Important in Education of Black Children. *Momentum,* 30-31.

Gay, G., & Abrahams, R. (1976). Black culture in the classroom. In R. Abrahams & R. Troike (Eds.), *Language and Cultural Diversity in American Education.* Englewood Cliffs: Prentice-Hall.

Gilbert, S., & Gay, G. (1984). Improving the Success in School of Poor Black Children. *Phi Delta Kappan,* 133-137.

Gitter, A., Black, H., & Mostofsky, D. (1972). Race and
sex in the perception of emotion. *Journal of Social
Issues, 28*, 63-78.

Guinagh, B. (1971). An experimental study of basic
learning ability and intelligence in low
socioeconomic status children. *Child Development,
42*, 27-36.

Hall, A., & Kaye, D. (1977). Patterns of early cognitive
development among boys in four sub cultural
groups. *Journal of Educational Psychology, 69*, 66-
87.

Hill, W., & Fox, W. (1973). Black and white marine squad
leader's perceptions of racially mixed squads.
Academy of Management Journal, 16, 680-686.

Keil, C. (1966). *Urban Blues.* Chicago: University of
Chicago Press.

Martinez, J. (1977). *Chicano Psychology.* New York:
Academic Press.

McClure, E. (1978). Teacher and pupil questions and responses and the Mexican-American child. *The Bilingual Review, 5*, 40-44.

Milburn, T. (2000). Inferring cultural learning styles - Puerto Ricans in the US. *ED448492.*

Morales-Jones, C. (1998). *Understanding Hispanic Culture: From Tolerance to Acceptance, 64*(4), 13-17.

Morris, M. (1981). *Saying and meaning in Puerto Rico: Some problems in the ethnography of discourse.* Oxford: Pergamon Press.

Ogbu, J. (1992). Adaptation to minority status and impact on school success. *Theory Into Practice, 31*(4), 287-295.

Orasanu, J., Lee, C., & Scribner, S. (1979). Free Recall: Ethnic and economic group comparisons. *Child Development, 50*, 1100-1109.

Ortiz, F. (1988). Hispanic-American children's experiences in classrooms: A comparison between Hispanic and non-Hispanic children. In L. Weis (Ed.), *Class, race, and gender in American education* (pp. 63-86). New York: State University of New York Press.

Patthey-Chavez, G. (1993). High school as an arena for cultural conflict and association for Latino Angelinos. *Anthropology & Educational Quarterly, 24*, 33-60.

Rubovits, P., & Maehr, M. (1973). Pygmalion Black and White. *Journal of Personality and Social Psychology, 25*, 261-267.

Rychlak, J. (1975). Affective assessment, intelligence, social class, and racial learning style. *Journal of Personality and Social Psychology, 32*, 989-995.

Shade, B. (1978). Social-Psychological Characteristics of Achieving Black Children. *The Negro Educational Review, 29*(2), 80-86.

Shade, B. (1997). The Culture and Style of Mexican-American Society. In B. Shade (Ed.), *Culture, Style, and the Educative Process: Making Schools Work for Racially Diverse Students.* Springfield, Ill: Charles C. Thomas.

Shade, B. (1997). African-American Cognitive Patterns: A review of the Research. In B. Shade (Ed.), *Making Schools Work for Racially Diverse Students.* Springfield, Ill.: Charles C. Thomas.

Shade, B. (1997). Culture and Learning Style within the African-American Community. In B. Shade (Ed.), *Culture, Style, and the Educative Process: Making Schools Work for Racially Diverse Students.* Springfield, Ill.: Charles C. Thomas.

Shade, B., Kelly, C., & Oberg, M. (1997). *Creating Culturally Responsive Classroom.* Washington, DC: American Psychological Association.

Sierra, V. (1973). Learning style of the Mexican American. In L. Bransford, L. Baca & K. Lane (Eds.), *Cultural Diversity and the Exceptional Child.* Reston: Council for Exceptional Children.

Sigel, I., Anderson, L., & Shapiro, H. (1966). Categorization behavior of lower and middle-class Negro preschool children. *Journal of Negro Education, 35*, 218-229.

Slavin, R. (1983). *Cooperative Learning.* New York: Longman Press.

St. John, N. (1971). Thirty-six teachers: Their characteristics, and outcomes for black and white pupils. *American Educational Research Journal, 8*, 635-648.

Witmer, J., & Ferinden, F. (1970). Perception of school climate: Comparison of black and white teachers within the same schools. *Journal of the Student Personnel Association for Teacher Education, 9*, 1-7.

Appendix D

Co-Developing Shared Vision Response Questions

1. How did the researcher implement the personal vision process?

2. How did the researcher ensure that all participants were treated equally?

3. How did the researcher encourage interdependence and diversity

4. How did the researcher recruit participants? Why?

5. How did the researcher ensure that all participants spoke for themselves?

6. How did the researcher nurture reverence for each participant?

7. How did the researcher build momentum?

8. How did the researcher ensure that there was dialogue during this meeting?

Appendix E

Autoethnography Response Questions

Those studied (participants) questions are:

1. How do teachers know that they are promoting positive racial teacher-student classroom relationships?

2. How do teachers perceive me as a promoter of positive racial teacher-student classroom relationships leadership?

3. How do I perceive teachers that promote positive teacher-student classroom relationships?

4. How do I perceive teachers that do not promote positive racial teacher-student classroom relationships?

Myself: (as qualitative inquirer)

1. How do I know that I am promoting positive racial teacher-student classroom relationships?

2. What values and beliefs do I have regarding promoting positive racial teacher-student classroom relationships?

3. What will I do with what I have found about promoting positive racial teacher-student classroom relationships?

Those receiving the study (audience):

1. How do my readers make sense of my promoting positive racial teacher-student classroom relationships leadership?

2. How do my readers perceive me as a promoter of positive racial teacher-student classroom relationships?

3. How do I perceive my readers?

Appendix F

Leadership Challenge Reflection Questions

Model the Way

1. What are my personal beliefs and values?

2. How do I build a consensus that aligns with my personal beliefs and values?

3. What examples do I set that align my personal values with shared values?

Inspire a Shared Vision

1. What vision do I have for my organization?

2. How do I enlist others to share in a common vision?

Challenge the Process

1. What innovative ways do I change, grow, and improve my organization?

2. What risks do I take that change, grow, and improve my organization?

3. What have I learned from my mistakes?

Enable Other to Act

1. How do I foster collaboration that promotes cooperative goals and builds trust?

2. How do I strengthen others by sharing power and discretion?

Encourage the Heart

1. How do I recognize contributions by showing appreciation for individual excellence?

2. How do I celebrate the values and victories that create a spirit of community?

Appendix G

Shared Vision Development

1. Imagine an occasion when you were involved in a
   positive teacher-student interaction in your
   classroom. Write down what happened.

_____

_____

_____

_____

_____

_____

_____

_____

_____

_____

_____

_____

_____

_____

_____

_____

2. Write your personal vision for promoting positive teacher-student classroom relationships?

_____

_____

_____

_____

_____

_____

_____

_____

_____

_____

_____

_____

_____

_____

2. Write your personal vision for promoting positive
   student classroom relationships?

Notes

Notes

Notes

Notes